The Story of Christmas

The Story of Christmas

GRAMERCY BOOKS
• New York •

This 1997 edition is published by Gramercy Books,
a division of Random House Value Publishing, Inc.,
201 East 50th Street, New York, New York 10022.

Gramercy Books and colophon are trademarks of
Random House Value Publishing, Inc.

Random House
New York • Toronto • London • Sydney • Auckland

Printed and bound in China

Compiled, edited, designed, and composited by
Frank J. Finamore

A CIP catalog record for this book is available from the Library of
Congress.

The Story of Christmas
ISBN 0–517–18358–7

8   7   6   5   4   3   2

❄ CONTENTS ❄

Christmas Cookie and Candy Recipes

❄ Preface ❄

There is perhaps no holiday more special than Christmas. With breathless anticipation every child awaits the Christmas season—no school, endless feasts of candies and cake, and piles of presents: it's like paradise on earth. While children may not completely understand the significance and subtleties of the holiday—the birth of Jesus Christ, the Son of God who died for our sins—they fully appreciate its spirit, and in their innocence more so than adults. And that spirit is joy. For the season symbolizes the promise and fulfillment of our humanity, as the birth of Jesus Christ is the salvation and glory of mankind.

In this ever-increasingly fast-paced modern society, the commercialization of the season has perhaps clouded the true meaning of Christmas. How many people have an old-fashioned Christmas anymore? Is a classic story like O. Henry's "Gifts of the Magi" too sentimental for this cynical age? Is the description of the family feast in Charles Dickens's "The Christmas Dinner" now a nostalgic fantasy, impossible to recreate today? Only for those who do not make the effort.

In our present era of technological marvels that have eased our lives—computers, jet planes, television, et al.—we have to try harder to find the true spirit of Christmas that our forebears took for granted. One has to realize that the joy of Christmas is always present, albeit bogged down or obscured by modern life. One just has to slow down and make the time to appreciate life, for Christmas is not merely about its celebration— the gifts, the food, or the revelry—but involves giving of oneself, as Christ did, to the people one loves, and to everyone.

This little book, *The Story of Christmas,* is a timeless reminder of Christmas past. It collects classic stories, poems, and carols, as well as recipes, that have stood the test of time. It will serve as an invaluable guide for its true celebration for your family for generations to come.

Frank James Finamore

New York
1997

Christmas Stories, Poems, and Carols

wrapped him in swaddling clothes, and laid him

The Birth of Jesus

❊ FROM THE NEW TESTAMENT ❊

*A*nd it came to pass in those days, that there went out a decree from Caesar Augustus, that all the world should be taxed. (And this taxing was first made when Cyrenius was governor of Syria.)

And all went to be taxed, everyone into his own city.

And Joseph also went up from Galilee, out of the city of Nazareth, into Judaea, unto the city of David, which is called Bethlehem; (because he was of the house and lineage of David.) to be taxed with Mary his espoused wife, being great with child.

And so it was, that, while they were there, the days were accomplished that she should be delivered.

And she brought forth her firstborn son, and wrapped him in swaddling clothes, and laid him in a manger, because there was no room for them in the inn.

LUKE 2:1–7

And it came to pass, as the angels were gone away from them into heaven, the shepherds said one to another, "Let us now go even unto Bethlehem, and see this thing which is come to pass, which the Lord hath made known unto us."

And they came with haste, and found Mary, and Joseph, and the babe lying in a manger.

And when they had seen it, they made known abroad the saying which was told them concerning this child.

And all they that heard it wondered at those things which were told them by the shepherds.

But Mary kept all these things, and pondered them in her heart.

And the shepherds returned, glorifying and praising God for all the things that they had heard and seen, as it was told unto them.

LUKE 2:15-20

Now when Jesus was born in Bethlehem of Judaea in the days of Herod the king, behold, there came wise men from the east to Jerusalem, saying, "Where is he that is born King of the Jews? for we have seen his star in the east, and are come to worship him."

When Herod the king had heard these things, he was troubled, and all Jerusalem with him. And when he had gathered all the chief priests and scribes of the people together, he demanded of them where Christ should be born.

And they said unto him, "In Bethlehem of Judaea: for thus it is written by the prophet, 'And thou Bethlehem, in the land of Judah, art not the least among the princes of Judah: for out of thee shall come a Governor, that shall rule my people Israel.'"

Then Herod, when he had privily called the wise men, inquired of them diligently what time the star appeared.

And he sent them to Bethlehem, and said, "Go and search diligently for the young child; and when ye have found him, bring me word again, that I may come and worship him also."

When they had heard the king, they departed; and, lo, the star, which they saw in the east, went before them, till it came and stood over where the young child was.

When they saw the star, they rejoiced with exceeding great joy.

And when they were come into the house, they saw the young child with Mary his mother, and fell down, and worshipped him: and when they had opened their treasures, they presented unto him gifts; gold, and frankincense, and myrrh.

And being warned of God in a dream that they should not return to Herod, they departed into their own country another way.

And when they were departed, behold, the angel

of the Lord appeared to Joseph in a dream, saying, "Arise, and take the young child and his mother, and flee into Egypt, and be thou there until I bring thee word: for Herod will seek the young child to destroy him."

When he arose, he took the young child and his mother by night, and departed into Egypt, and was there until the death of Herod; that it might be fulfilled which was spoken of the Lord by the prophet, saying, "Out of Egypt have I called my son."

Then Herod, when he saw that he was mocked of the wise men, was exceeding wroth, and sent forth, and slew all the children that were in Bethlehem, and in all the coasts thereof, from two years old and under, according to the time which he had diligently inquired of the wise men.

Then was fulfilled that which was spoken by Jeremy the prophet, saying, "In Rama was there a voice heard, lamentation, and weeping, and great mourning, Rachel weeping for her children, and would not be comforted, because they are not."

MATTHEW 2:1–18

Gifts of the Magi

❄ O. HENRY ❄

One dollar and eighty-seven cents. That was all. And sixty cents of it was in pennies. Pennies saved one and two at a time by bulldozing the grocer and the vegetable man and the butcher until one's cheeks burned with the silent imputation of parsimony that such close dealing implied. Three times Della counted it. One dollar and eighty-seven cents. And the next day would be Christmas.

There was clearly nothing to do but flop down on the shabby little couch and howl. So Della did it. Which instigates the moral reflection that life is made up of sobs, sniffles, and smiles, with sniffles predominating. While the mistress of the home is gradually subsiding from the first stage to the second, take a look at the home. A furnished flat at eight dollars per week. It did not exactly beggar description, but it certainly had that word on the lookout for the mendicancy squad.

In the vestibule below was a letter box into which no letter would go, and an electric button from which no mortal finger could coax a ring.

Also appertaining thereunto was a card bearing the name "Mr. James Dillingham Young."

The "Dillingham" had been flung to the breeze during a former period of prosperity when its possessor was being paid thirty dollars per week. Now, when the income was shrunk to twenty dollars, the letters of "Dillingham" looked blurred, as though they were thinking seriously of contracting to a modest and unassuming D. But whenever Mr. James Dillingham Young came home and reached his flat above he was called "Jim" and greatly hugged by Mrs. James Dillingham Young, already introduced to you as Della. Which is all very good.

Della finished her cry and attended to her cheeks with the powder rag. She stood by the window and looked out dully at a gray cat walking a gray fence in a gray backyard. Tomorrow would be Christmas Day, and she had only one dollar and eighty-seven cents with which to buy Jim a present. She had been saving every penny she could for months, with this result. Twenty dollars a week doesn't go far. Expenses had been greater than she had calculated. They always are. Only one dollar and eighty-seven cents to buy a present for Jim. Her Jim. Many a happy hour she had spent planning for something nice for him. Something fine and rare and sterling— something just a little bit near to being worthy of the honor of being owned by Jim.

There was a pier glass between the windows of the room. Perhaps you have seen a pier glass in an eight-dollar flat. A very thin and very agile person may, by observing his reflection in a rapid sequence of longitudinal strips, obtain a fairly accurate conception of his looks. Della, being slender, had mastered the art.

Suddenly she whirled from the window and stood before the glass. Her eyes were shining brilliantly, but her face had lost its color within twenty seconds. Rapidly she pulled down her hair and let it fall to its full length.

Now, there were two possessions of the James Dillingham Youngs in which they both took a mighty pride. One was Jim's gold watch that had been his father's and grandfather's. The other was Della's hair. Had the Queen of Sheba lived in the flat across the air shaft, Della would have let her hair hang out the window some day to dry just to depreciate her majesty's jewels and gifts. Had King Solomon been the janitor, with all his treasures piled up in the basement, Jim would have pulled out his watch every time he passed, just to see him pluck at his beard from envy.

So now Della's beautiful hair fell about her, rippling and shining like a cascade of brown waters. It reached below her knee and made itself almost a garment for her. And then she did it up again nervously and quickly. Once she faltered for a minute and stood still while a tear or two splashed on the worn red carpet.

On went her old brown jacket; on went her old brown hat. With a whirl of skirts and with the brilliant sparkle still in her eyes, she fluttered out the door and down the stairs to the street.

Where she stopped the sign read: "Mme. Sofronie. Hair Goods of All Kinds." One flight up Della ran, and collected herself, panting. Madame, large, too white, chilly, hardly looked the "Sofronie."

"Will you buy my hair?" asked Della.

"I buy hair," said Madame. "Take yer hat off and let's have a sight at the looks of it."

Down rippled the brown cascade.

"Twenty dollars," said Madame, lifting the mass with a practiced hand.

"Give it to me quick," said Della.

Oh, and the next two hours tripped by on rosy wings. Forget the hashed metaphor. She was ransacking the stores for Jim's present.

She found it at last. It surely had been made for Jim and no one else. There was no other like it in any of the stores, and she had turned all of them inside out. It was a platinum fob chain simple and chaste in design, properly proclaiming its value by substance alone and not by meretricious ornamentation—as all good things should do. It was even worthy of The Watch. As soon as she saw it she knew that it must be Jim's. It was like him. Quietness and value—the description applied to both. Twenty-one dollars they took from her for it, and she hurried home with the eighty-seven cents. With that chain on his watch Jim might be properly anxious about the time in any company. Grand as the watch was, he sometimes looked at it on the sly on account of the old leather strap that he used in place of a chain.

When Della reached home her intoxication gave way a little to prudence and reason. She got out her curling irons and lighted the gas and went to work repairing the ravages made by generosity added to love. Which is always a tremendous task, dear friends—a mammoth task.

Within forty minutes her head was covered with tiny, close-lying curls that made her look wonderfully like a truant schoolboy. She looked at her reflection in the mirror long, carefully, and critically.

"If Jim doesn't kill me," she said to herself, "before he takes a second look at me, he'll say I look like a Coney Island chorus girl. But what could I do—oh! what could I do with a dollar and eighty-seven cents?"

At seven o'clock the coffee was made and the frying pan was on the back of the stove and ready to cook the chops.

Jim was never late. Della doubled the fob chain in her hand and sat on the corner of the table near the door that he always entered. Then she heard his step on the stairway down on the first flight, and she turned white for just a moment. She had a habit of saying little silent prayers about the simplest everyday things, and now she whispered: "Please God, make him think I am still pretty."

The door opened and Jim stepped in and closed it. He looked thin and very serious. Poor fellow, he was only twenty-two—and to be burdened with a family! He needed a new overcoat and he was without gloves.

Jim stopped inside the door, as immovable as a setter at the scent of quail. His eyes were fixed upon Della and there was an expression in them that she could not read, and it terrified her. It was not anger, nor surprise, nor disapproval, nor horror, nor any of the sentiments that she had been prepared for. He simply stared at her fixedly with that peculiar expression on his face.

Della wriggled off the table and went for him.

"Jim, darling," she cried, "don't look at me that way. I had my hair cut off and sold it because I couldn't have lived through Christmas without giving you a present. It'll grow out again—you won't mind, will you? I just had to do it. My hair grows awfully fast. Say 'Merry Christmas!' Jim, and let's be happy. You don't know what a nice—what a beautiful, nice gift I've got for you."

"You've cut off your hair?" asked Jim, laboriously, as if he had not arrived at that patent fact yet even after the hardest mental labor.

"Cut it off and sold it," said Della. "Don't you like me just as well, anyhow? I'm me without my hair, ain't I?"

Jim looked about the room curiously.

"You say your hair is gone?" he said, with an air almost of idiocy.

"You needn't look for it," said Della. "It's sold, I tell you—sold and gone, too. It's Christmas Eve, boy. Be good to me, for it went for you. Maybe the hairs of my head were numbered," she went on with a sudden serious sweetness, "but nobody could ever count my love for you. Shall I put the chops on, Jim?"

Out of his trance Jim seemed quickly to wake. He enfolded his Della. For ten seconds let us regard with discreet scrutiny some inconsequential object in the other direction. Eight dollars a week or a million a year—what is the difference? A mathematician or a wit would give you the wrong answer. The magi brought valuable gifts, but that was not among them. This dark assertion will be illuminated later on.

Jim drew a package from his overcoat pocket and threw it upon the table.

"Don't make any mistake, Dell," he said, "about me. I don't think there's anything in the way of a haircut or a shave or a shampoo that could make me like my girl any less. But if you'll unwrap that package you may see why you had me going a while at first."

White fingers and nimble tore at the string and paper. And then an ecstatic scream of joy; and then, alas! a quick feminine change to hysterical tears and wails, necessitating the immediate employment of all the comforting powers of the lord of the flat.

For there lay The Combs—the set of combs, side and back, that Della had worshipped for long in a Broadway window. Beautiful combs, pure tortoise shell, with jeweled rims—just the shade to wear in the beautiful vanished hair. They were expensive combs, she knew, and her heart had simply craved and yearned over them without the least hope of possession. And now, they were hers, but the tresses that should have adorned the coveted adornments were gone.

But she hugged them to her bosom, and at length she was able to look up with dim eyes and a smile and say: "My hair grows so fast, Jim!"

And then Della leaped up like a little singed cat and cried, "Oh, oh!"

Jim had not yet seen his beautiful present. She held it out to him eagerly upon her open palm. The dull precious metal seemed to flash with a reflection of her bright and ardent spirit.

"Isn't it a dandy, Jim? I hunted all over town to find it. You'll have to look at the time a hundred times a day now. Give me your watch I want to see how it looks on it."

Instead of obeying, Jim tumbled down on the couch and put his hands under the back of his head and smiled.

"Dell," said he, "let's put our Christmas presents away and keep 'em a while. They're too nice to use just at present. I sold the watch to get the money to buy your combs. And now suppose you put the chops on."

The magi, as you know, were wise men—wonderfully wise men who brought gifts to the Babe in the manger. They invented the art of giving Christmas presents. Being wise, their gifts were no doubt wise ones, possibly bearing the privilege of exchange in case of duplication. And here I have lamely related to you the uneventful chronicle of two foolish children in a flat who most unwisely sacrificed for each other the greatest treasures of their house. But, in a last word to the wise of these days, let it be said that of all who give gifts these two were the wisest. Of all who give and receive gifts, such as they are wisest. Everywhere they are wisest. They are the magi.

The Legend of Saint Nicholas

❉ GEORGENE FAULKNER ❉

*O*nce upon a time there lived in Myra a good man named Nicholas. When he was a young man his father and mother died of the plague, and he was left the sole heir of all their vast estate. But he looked upon all this money as belonging to God and felt that he, himself, was merely the steward of God's mercies. So he went about everywhere doing good and sharing his riches with all those who were in need.

Now, there lived in that country a certain nobleman who had three beautiful daughters. He had been very rich, but he lost all his property and became so poor that he did not know what to do to provide for his family. His daughters were anxious to be married, but their father had no money to give them dowries and, in that country, no maiden could marry unless she had her marriage portion, or dowry. They were so very poor that they had scarcely enough food to eat. Their clothes were so worn and ragged that they would not go out of the house and their father was overcome with shame and sorrow.

When the good Nicholas heard of their troubles he longed to help them. He knew that the father was proud and that it would be hard to give him money; so he thought that it would be best to surprise them with a gift. Then Nicholas took some gold and, tying it in a long silken purse, went at once to the home of the poor nobleman. It was night and the beautiful maidens were fast asleep while the broken-hearted father, too wretched to go to bed, sat by the fireside watching and praying.

Nicholas stood outside, wondering how he could bestow his gift without being seen, when suddenly the moon came from behind the clouds and he saw that a window in the house was open. Creeping softly to the open window, he threw the purse right into the room where it fell at the feet of the nobleman. The father picked up the purse and was very surprised to find it full of gold pieces.

Awakening his daughters the father said, "See this purse which came through the window and fell at my feet. It is indeed a gift from Heaven. God has remembered us in our time of need."

After they had rejoiced together, they agreed to give most of the gold to the eldest daughter, so that she would have her dowry and could wed the young man she loved.

Not long after that, Nicholas filled another silken purse with gold and again he went by night so that no one should see him, and he threw this purse, too, through the open window. When the father saw this golden gift he again gave thanks. The money he gave to the second daughter who, like her sister, at once married the man of her choice.

Meanwhile the father was curious to find out who was so kind to them, for he wished to thank the person who had come in the night to help them with these golden gifts. So he watched and waited night after night. And after a time the good Nicholas came with another silken purse filled with gold pieces for the youngest daughter.

He was just about to throw it into the room when the nobleman rushed from the house and, seizing him by his long robe, knelt before him, saying, "Oh good Nicholas, servant of God, why seek to hide thyself?" And he kissed his hands and feet and tried to thank him.

But Nicholas answered, "Do not thank me, my good man, but thank the Heavenly Father who has sent me to you in answer to your prayers. I am only His messenger to help those who trust in Him. Tell no man of these gifts of gold, nor who brought them to you in the night, for my deeds are done in His name."

Thus the youngest daughter of the nobleman was married, and she and her father and sisters all lived happily the rest of their lives.

The good Nicholas went about from place to place, and wherever he went he did deeds of kindness, so that all the people loved him.

One time he took a long journey to the Holy Land, and when he was upon the sea there came a terrible storm, so that the ship was tossed about and almost wrecked, and all the sailors gave up hope.

But the good Nicholas said, "Fear not, our Heavenly Father will bring us safely into harbor." Then he knelt and prayed to God and the storm ceased and the boat was brought safely to the land. Whereupon the sailors fell at the feet of Nicholas and thanked him.

He answered them humbly, "Thank your Father who is in Heaven, for He is the ruler of us all. It is He who rules the earth and the sky and the sea, and who, in His good mercy, spared our lives that we may serve Him."

When Nicholas returned from Palestine he went to the city of Myra, where he was appointed a bishop. After that he preached God's Word and went about doing good all of his life. When he died the people said, "We will not call him Bishop Nicholas, but we will call him Saint Nicholas, for if ever there was a saint upon earth it was our good Nicholas." And so to this day he is called Good Saint Nicholas.

And now in many countries they tell the story of the good Saint Nicholas, and how he goes about the earth at Christmas time bringing gifts of love to all who deserve them, and, because he had put his gifts of gold in long silken purses, today children hang up their long stockings to hold his gifts. And when the children are very good he fills their stockings with sweets and toys and trinkets, but if they have been naughty, they will find a bunch of switches, showing that they deserve to be punished.

We all know that on Christmas Eve Saint Nicholas will come in the night, for he never likes to be seen. And we know that he will always live—for he is the spirit of love and love can never die.

So, every Christmas, let us give our gifts as he did those silken purses so long ago—without anyone knowing about it—and let our gifts be a surprise. Then we, too, can have the spirit of love and join in this celebration of Christmas with good Saint Nicholas.

Is There a Santa Claus?

In September 1871 eight-year-old Virginia Hanlon of West 95th Street in New York City wrote the following letter to *The New York Sun:*

> *Dear Editor,*
> *I am eight years old. Some of my friends say there is no Santa Claus. Papa says, "If you see it in the* Sun, *it's so." Please tell me the truth, Is there a Santa Claus?*

In one of the most famous editorials ever written, the editors replied:

Virginia, your little friends are wrong. They have been affected by the skepticism of a skeptical age. They do not believe except what they see. They think that nothing can be which is not comprehensible by their little minds. All minds, Virginia, whether they be men's or children's, are little. In this great universe of ours man is a mere insect, an ant, in his intellect, as compared with the boundless world about him, as measured by the intelligence capable of grasping the whole of truth and knowledge.

Yes, Virginia, there is a Santa Claus. He exists as certainly as love and generosity and devotion exist, and you know that they abound and give to your life its highest beauty and joy. Alas! how dreary would be the world if there were no Santa Claus! It would be as dreary as if there were no Virginias. There would be no childlike faith, no poetry, no romance to make tolerable this existence. We should have no enjoyment, except in sense and sight. The eternal light with which childhood fills the world would be extinguished.

Not believe in Santa Claus! You might as well not believe in fairies! You might get your papa to hire men to watch in all the chimneys on Christmas Eve to catch Santa Claus, but even if they did not see Santa Claus come down, what would that prove? Nobody sees Santa Claus, but that is no sign that there is no Santa Claus. The most real things in the world are those that neither children nor men can see. Did you ever see fairies dancing on the lawn? Of course not, but that's no proof that they are not there. Nobody can conceive or imagine all the wonders there are unseen and unseeable in the world.

You tear apart the baby's rattle and see what makes the noise inside, but there is a veil covering the unseen world which not the strongest man, nor even the united strength of all the strongest men that ever lived, could tear apart. Only faith, fancy, poetry, love, romance can push aside that curtain and view and picture the supernal beauty and glory beyond. Is it all real? Ah, Virginia, in all this world there is nothing else real and abiding.

No Santa Claus! Thank God he lives, and he lives forever. A thousand years from now, Virginia, nay, ten times ten thousand years from now, he will continue to make glad the heart of childhood.

From St. Nicholas Magazine

Santa Claus lives somewhere near the North Pole, so he can't be interfered with. It is the only place where he can be sure of not being overrun with callers, who would take up all his time, and prevent him from getting his Christmas budget ready—by no means a light piece of work. As to how he makes up his load of toys, it is certainly curious; but it is his business not ours. He uses reindeer to draw his sleigh because no other animals can endure the climate in which their master must live. Just what Santa looks like is not altogether certain, but there is a belief among the children who have sat up to receive his visits that he is not so big but that he can get through an ordinary chimney; that he is compelled to dress in furs because of the cold ride through the long winter night; that he looks good-natured because no one that loves young folk can help looking so; and that his beard and his hair are white because he is older by some years than he was in his younger days. He must be a jolly and kindly old gentleman, for otherwise he wouldn't be giving out his toys in that sly, queer way of his—after the little ones are fast asleep and snug in their beds. Oh, we can tell quite a number of things about his tricks and his manners! But don't sit up for him; he doesn't like it. He loses valuable time when he is compelled to dodge the prying eyes of little Susan Sly and Master Paul Pry, and so kindly an old fellow should not be bothered. Just go to bed, close your eyes up good and tight, and—see what you will find in the morning!

The Christmas Dinner

❄ CHARLES DICKENS ❄

Christmas time! The man must be a misanthrope indeed, in whose breast something like a jovial feeling is not roused—in whose mind some pleasant associations are not awakened—by the recurrence of Christmas. There are people who will tell you that Christmas is not to them what it used to be: that each succeeding Christmas has found some cherished hope, or happy prospect, of the year before, dimmed or passed away, and that the present only serves to remind them of reduced circumstances and straitened incomes—of the feasts they once bestowed on hollow friends, and of the cold looks that meet them now, in adversity and misfortune. Never heed such dismal reminiscences. There are few men who have lived long enough in the world, who cannot call up such thoughts any day in the year. Then do not select the merriest of the three hundred and sixty-five, for your doleful recollections, but draw your chair nearer the blazing fire—fill the glass and send round the song—and if your room be smaller than it was a dozen years ago, or if your glass be filled with reeking punch, instead of sparkling wine, put a good face on the matter, and empty it offhand, and fill another, and troll off the old ditty you used to sing, and thank God it's no worse. Look on the merry faces of your children as they sit round the fire. One little seat may be empty; one slight form that gladdened the father's heart, and roused the mother's pride to look upon, may not be there. Dwell not upon the past; think not that one short year ago, the fair child now resolving into dust, sat before you, with the bloom of health upon its cheek, and the gay unconsciousness of infancy in its joyous eye. Reflect upon your present blessings— of which every man has many—not on your past misfortunes, of which all men have some. Fill your glass again, with a merry face and contented heart. Our life on it, but your Christmas shall be merry, and your New Year a happy one.

Who can be insensible to the outpourings of good feeling, and the honest interchange of affectionate attachment, which abound at this season of the year? A Christmas family party! We know nothing in nature more delightful! There seems a magic in the very name of Christmas. Petty jealousies and discords are forgotten: social feelings are awakened in bosoms to which they have long been strangers: father and son, or brother and sister, who have met and passed with averted gaze, or a look of cold recognition, for months before, proffer and return the cordial embrace, and bury their past animosities in their present happiness. Kindly hearts that have yearned towards each other, but have been withheld by false notions of pride and self-dignity, are again reunited, and all is kindness and benevolence! Would that Christmas lasted the whole year through, and that the prejudices and passions which deform our better nature, were never called into action among those to whom they should ever be strangers!

The Christmas family party that we mean, is not a mere assemblage of relations, got up at a week or two's notice, originating this year, having no family precedent in the last, and not likely to be repeated in the next. It is an annual gathering of all the accessible members of the family, young or old, rich or poor; and all the children look forward to it, for two months beforehand, in a fever of anticipation. Formerly it was held at Grandpapa's; but Grandpapa getting old, and Grandmamma getting old too, and rather infirm, they have given up housekeeping, and domesticated themselves with Uncle George, so the party always takes place at Uncle George's house, but Grandmamma sends in most of the good things, and Grandpapa always will toddle down, all the way to Newgate market, to buy the turkey, which he engages a porter to bring home behind him in triumph, always insisting on the man's being rewarded with a glass of spirits, over and above his hire, to drink "a merry Christmas and a happy New Year" to Aunt George. As to Grandmamma, she is very secret and mysterious for two or three days beforehand, but not sufficiently so to prevent rumors getting afloat that she has purchased a beautiful new cap with pink ribbons for each of the servants, together with sundry books, and penknives, and pencil cases, for the younger branches; to say nothing of diverse secret additions to the order originally given by Aunt George at the pastry cook's, such as another dozen of mince pies for the dinner, and a large plum cake for the children.

On Christmas Eve, Grandmamma is always in excellent spirits, and after employing all the children, during the day, in stoning the plums and all that, insists regularly every year on Uncle George coming down into the kitchen, taking off his coat, and stirring the pudding for half an hour or so, which Uncle George good-humoredly does, to the vociferous delight of the children and servants, and the evening concludes with a glorious game of blind-man's-bluff, in an early stage of which Grandpapa takes great care to be caught, in order that he may have an opportunity of displaying his dexterity.

On the following morning, the old couple, with as many of the children as the pew will hold, go to church in great state, leaving Aunt George at home dusting decanters and filling castors, and Uncle George carrying bottles into the dining-parlor, and calling for corkscrews, and getting into everybody's way.

When the church party return to lunch, Grandpapa produces a small sprig of mistletoe from his pocket, and tempts the boys to kiss their little cousins under it—a proceeding which affords both the boys and the old gentleman unlimited satisfaction, but which rather outrages Grandmamma's ideas of decorum, until Grandpapa says, that when he was just thirteen years and three months old, he kissed Grandmamma under a mistletoe too, on which the children clap their hands, and laugh very heartily, as do Aunt George and Uncle George; and Grandmamma looks pleased, and says, with a benevolent smile, that Grandpapa always was an impudent dog, on which the children laugh very heartily again, and Grandpapa more heartily than any of them.

But all these diversions are nothing to the subsequent excitement when Grandmamma in a high cap, and slate-colored silk gown, and Grandpapa with a beautifully plaited shirt-frill, and white neckerchief, seat themselves on one side of the drawing-room fire, with Uncle George's children and little cousins innumerable, seated in the front, waiting the arrival of the anxiously expected visitors. Suddenly a hackney coach is heard to stop, and Uncle George, who has been looking out of the window, exclaims, "Here's Jane!" on which the children rush to the door, and helter-skelter downstairs; and Uncle Robert and Aunt Jane, and the dear little baby, and the nurse, and the whole party, are ushered upstairs amidst tumultuous shouts of "Oh, my!" from the children, and frequently repeated warnings not to hurt baby from the nurse: and Grandpapa takes the child, and Grandmamma kisses her daughter, and the confusion of this first entry has scarcely subsided, when some other aunts and uncles with more cousins arrive, and the grown-up cousins flirt with each other, and so do the little cousins too, for that matter, and nothing is to be heard but a confused din of talking, laughing, and merriment.

A hesitating double knock at the street door, heard during a momentary pause in the conversation, excites inquiry of "Who's that?" and two or three children, who have been standing at the window, announce in a low voice, that it's "poor Aunt Margaret." Upon which Aunt George leaves the room to welcome the newcomer, and Grandmamma draws herself up rather stiff and stately, for Margaret married a poor man without her consent, and poverty not being a sufficiently weighty punishment for her offense has been discarded by her friends, and debarred the society of her dearest relatives.

But Christmas has come round, and the unkind feelings that have struggled against better dispositions during the year, have melted away before its genial influence, like half-formed ice beneath the morning sun. It is not difficult in a moment of angry feeling for a parent to denounce a disobedient child; but to banish her at a period of general goodwill and hilarity, from the hearth round which she has sat on so many anniversaries of the same day, expanding by slow degrees from infancy to girlhood, and then bursting, almost imperceptibly, into the high-spirited and beautiful woman, is widely different. The air of conscious rectitude, and cold forgiveness, which the old lady has assumed, sits ill upon her; and when the poor girl is led in by her sister, pale in looks and broken in spirit—not from poverty, for that she could bear, but from the consciousness of undeserved neglect, and unmerited unkindness—it is easy to see how much of it is assumed. A momentary pause succeeds; the girl breaks suddenly from her sister and throws herself, sobbing, on her mother's neck. The father steps hastily forward, and grasps her husband's hand. Friends crowd round to offer their hearty congratulations, and happiness and harmony again prevail.

As to the dinner, it's perfectly delightful—nothing goes wrong, and everybody is in the very best of spirits, and disposed to please and be pleased. Grandpapa relates a circumstantial account of the purchase of the turkey, with a slight digression relative to the purchase of previous turkeys, on former Christmas days, which Grandmamma corroborates in the minutest particular. Uncle George tells stories, and carves poultry, and takes wine, and jokes with the children at the side table, and winks at the cousins that are making love, or being made love to, and exhilarates everybody with his good humor and hospitality; and when at last a stout servant staggers in with a gigantic pudding, with a sprig of holly in the top, there is such a laughing, and shouting, and clapping of little chubby hands, and kicking up of fat dumpy legs, as can only be equaled by the applause with which the astonishing feat of pouring lighted brandy into mince pies is received by the younger visitors. Then the desert!—and the wine!—and the fun!

Such beautiful speeches, and such songs, from Aunt Margaret's husband, who turns out to be such a nice man, and so attentive to Grandmamma! Even Grandpapa not only sings his annual song with unprecedented vigor, but on being honored with an unanimous encore, according to annual custom, actually comes out with a new one which nobody but Grandmamma ever heard before: and a young scape-grace of a cousin, who has been in some disgrace with the old people, for certain heinous sins of omission and commission—neglecting to call, and persisting in drinking Burton Ale—astonishes everybody into convulsions of laughter by volunteering the most extraordinary comic songs that were ever heard. And thus the evening passes, in a strain of rational goodwill and cheerfulness, doing more to awaken the sympathies of every member of the party in behalf of his neighbor, and to perpetuate their good feeling during the ensuing year, than all the homilies that have ever been written, by all the divines that have ever lived.

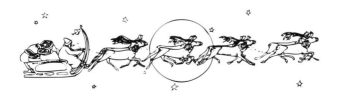

A Christmas Prayer

❄ ROBERT LOUIS STEVENSON ❄

*L*oving Father, help us remember the birth of Jesus, that we may share in the song of the angels, the gladness of the shepherds, and the worship of the wise men.

Close the door of hate and open the door of love all over the world.

Let kindness come with every gift and good desires with every greeting.

Deliver us from evil by the blessing which Christ brings, and teach us to be merry with clear hearts.

May the Christmas morning make us happy to be thy children, and the Christmas evening bring us to our beds with grateful thoughts, forgiving and forgiven, for Jesus' sake. Amen!

The Angel's Story

Through the blue and frosty heavens
   Christmas stars were shining bright;
Glistening lamps throughout the city
   Almost matched their gleaming light;
While the winter snow was lying,
And the winter winds were sighing,
   Long ago, one Christmas night.

While from every tower and steeple
   Pealing bells were sounding clear,
(Never were such tones of gladness
   Save when Christmas time is near),
Many a one that night was merry
   Who had toiled through all the year.

That night saw old wrongs forgiven,
   Friends, long parted, reconciled;
Voices all unused to laughter,
   Mournful eyes that rarely smiled,
Trembling hearts that feared the morrow,
   From their anxious thoughts beguiled.

Rich and poor felt love and blessing
   From the gracious season fall;

Joy and plenty in the cottage,
  Peace and feasting in the hall;
And the voices of the children
  Ringing clear above it all!

ADELAIDE ANNE PROCTER

A Visit from St. Nicholas

'Twas the night before Christmas, when all through
  the house
Not a creature was stirring, not even a mouse.
The stockings were hung by the chimney with care,
In hopes that St. Nicholas soon would be there.
The children were nestled all snug in their beds,
While visions of sugarplums danced in their heads;
And mamma in her kerchief, and I in my cap,
Had just settled our brains for a long winter's nap—
When out on the lawn there arose such a clatter,
I sprang from my bed to see what was the matter.
Away to the window I flew like a flash,
Tore open the shutters and threw up the sash.
The moon, on the breast of the new-fallen snow,
Gave a luster of midday to objects below;
When what to my wondering eyes should appear,
But a miniature sleigh and eight tiny reindeer,
With a little old driver, so lively and quick

I knew in a moment it must be St. Nick.
More rapid than eagles his coursers they came,
And he whistled and shouted and called them by
    name:
"Now, Dasher! now, Dancer! now, Prancer and
    Vixen!
On, Comet! on, Cupid! on, Donder and Blitzen!
To the top of the porch, to the top of the wall!
Now dash away, dash away, dash away all!"
As dry leaves that before the wild hurricane fly,
When they meet with an obstacle, mount to the sky,
So, up to the housetop the coursers they flew,
With a sleigh full of toys—and St. Nicholas too.
And then in a twinkling I heard on the roof
The prancing and pawing of each little hoof.
As I drew in my head and was turning around,
Down the chimney St. Nicholas came with a bound.

He was dressed all in fur from his head to his foot,
And his clothes were all tarnished with ashes and
    soot;
A bundle of toys he had flung on his back,
And he looked like a peddler just opening his pack.
His eyes, how they twinkled! his dimples, how
    merry!
His cheeks were like roses, his nose like a cherry;
His droll little mouth was drawn up like a bow,
And the beard on his chin was as white as the snow.
The stump of a pipe he held tight in his teeth,
And the smoke, it encircled his head like a wreath.
He had a broad face, and a little round belly

That shook, when he laughed, like a bowl full of
   jelly.
He was chubby and plump—a right jolly old elf—
And I laughed when I saw him, in spite of myself.
A wink of his eye and a twist of his head
Soon gave me to know I had nothing to dread.
He spoke not a word, but went straight to his work,
And filled all the stockings; then turned with a jerk,
And laying his finger aside of his nose,
And giving a nod, up the chimney he rose.
He sprang to his sleigh, to his team gave a whistle,
And away they all flew like the down of a thistle;
But I heard him exclaim, ere he drove out of sight:
Happy Christmas to all, and to all a good night!

CLEMENT C. MOORE

Christmas Day

A baby is a harmless thing,
   And wins our heart with one accord,
And Flower of Babies was their King,
   Jesus Christ our Lord:
Lily of lilies He
   Upon His Mother s knee;
Rose of roses, soon to be
   Crowned with thorns on leafless tree.

A lamb is innocent and mild,
    And merry on the soft green sod;
And Jesus Christ, the Undefiled,
    Is the Lamb of God:
Only spotless He
    Upon His Mother's knee;
White and ruddy, soon to be
    Sacrificed for you and me.

Nay, lamb is not so sweet a word,
    Nor lily half so pure a name;
Another name our hearts hath stirred,
    Kindling them to flame:
"Jesus" certainly
    Is music and melody:
Heart with heart in harmony
    Carol we and worship we.

CHRISTINA ROSSETTI

Joy to the World

Joy to the world! The Lord is come:
    Let earth receive her King.
Let ev'ry heart prepare Him room,
    And heaven and nature sing,
    And heaven and nature sing,
    And heaven and heaven and nature sing.

He rules the world with truth and grace,
    And makes the nations prove
The glories of His righteousness
    And wonders of His love,
    And wonders of His love,
    And wonders, wonders of His love.

Deck the Hall

Deck the hall with boughs of holly,
    Fa la la la la, la la la la.
'Tis the season to be jolly,
    Fa la la la la, la la la la.
Don we now our gay apparel,
    Fa la la la la, la la la la.
Troll the ancient Yuletide carol,

Fa la la la la, la la la la.
See the blazing yule before us,
   Fa la la la la, la la la la.
Strike the harp and join the chorus.
   Fa la la la la, la la la la.
Follow me in merry measure,
   Fa la la la la, la la la la.
While I tell of Yuletide treasure,
   Fa la la la la, la la la la.

Fast away the old year passes,
   Fa la la la la, la la la la.
Hail the new, ye lads and lasses,
   Fa la la la la, la la la la.
Sing we joyous, all together,
   Fa la la la la, la la la la.
Heedless of the wind and weather,
   Fa la la la la, la la la la.

Hark! The Herald Angels Sing

Hark! the herald angels sing,
"Glory to the newborn King!
Peace on earth, and mercy mild,
God and sinners reconciled."
Joyful, all ye nations, rise,
Join the triumph of the skies;
With th' angelic host proclaim,
"Christ is born in Bethlehem."
Hark! the herald angels sing,
"Glory to the newborn King!"

Christ, by highest heav'n adored:
Christ thee e'rlasting Lord;
Late in time behold him come,
Offspring of the favored one.
Veil'd in flesh, the Godhead see;
Hail, th' incarnate Deity:
Pleased, as man, with men to dwell,
Jesus, our Immanuel!
Hark! the herald angels sing,
"Glory to the newborn King!"

Hail! the heav'n-born Prince of peace!
Hail! the Son of Righteousness!
Light and life to all he brings,

Risen with healing in his wings
Mild he lays his glory by,
Born that man no more may die:
Born to raise the sons of earth,
Born to give them second birth.
Hark! the herald angels sing,
"Glory to the newborn King!"

O Little Town of Bethlehem

O little town of Bethlehem.
   How still we see thee lie;
Above thy deep and dreamless sleep
   The silent stars go by;
Yet in thy dark streets shineth
   The everlasting light.
The hopes and fears of all the years
   Are met in thee tonight.

For Christ is born of Mary,
   And gathered all above,
While mortals sleep the angels keep
   Their watch of wond'ring love.
O morning stars, together
   Proclaim the holy birth!
And praises sing to God the King,
   And peace to men on earth!

O Come, All Ye Faithful

O come, all ye faithful,
  Joyful and triumphant,
O come ye, O come ye to Bethlehem.
  Come and behold Him,
Monarch of Angels!
  O come, let us adore Him,
  O come, let us adore Him,
  O come, let us adore Him,
    Christ the Lord.

Sing, alleluia,
  All ye choirs of angels;
O sing, all ye blissful ones of Heaven above.
  Glory to God—
In the highest glory!
  O come, let us adore Him,
  O come, let us adore Him,
  O come, let us adore Him,
    Christ the Lord.

Yea, Lord, we greet Thee,
  Born this happy morning;
Jesus, to Thee be the glory giv'n;
  Word of the Father,
Now in the flesh appearing

O come, let us adore Him,
O come, let us adore Him,
O come, let us adore Him,
Christ the Lord.

Silent Night

Silent night, holy night!
   All is calm, all is bright.
Round yon Virgin, Mother and Child.
   Holy infant so tender and mild,
Sleep in heavenly peace,
   Sleep in heavenly peace.

Silent night, holy night!
   Shepherds quake at the sight.
Glories stream from heaven afar
   Heavenly hosts sing Alleluia,
Christ the Savior is born!
   Christ the Savior is born.

Silent night, holy night!
   Son of God love s pure light.
Radiant beams from Thy holy face
   With the dawn of redeeming grace,
Jesus Lord, at Thy birth.
   Jesus Lord at Thy birth.

We Wish You a Merry Christmas

We wish you a Merry Christmas,
We wish you a Merry Christmas,
We wish you a Merry Christmas,
   And a Happy New Year.

Good tidings to you,
And all of your kin,
Good tidings for Christmas,
And a Happy New Year.

We all know that Santa's coming,
We all know that Santa's coming.
We all know that Santa's coming,
   And soon will be here.

Good tidings to you,
And all of your kin,
Good tidings for Christmas,
And a Happy New Year.

We wish you a Merry Christmas,
We wish you a Merry Christmas,
We wish you a Merry Christmas,
   And a Happy New Year.

Christmas Cookie and Candy Recipes

Lebküchen

These spicy honey cookies have been part of the German Christmas tradition for hundreds of years. There are many recipes for lebküchen. This is one of the best. Makes about 90 cookies.

>   1 *cup honey*
>   2 *eggs*
> $\frac{3}{4}$ *cup firmly packed dark brown sugar*
>   1 *tablespoon lemon juice*
>   1 *teaspoon grated lemon rind*
> $2\frac{3}{4}$ *cups all-purpose flour*
> $1\frac{1}{2}$ *teaspoons baking soda*
>   1 *teaspoon ground cinnamon*
>   1 *teaspoon ground allspice*
> $\frac{1}{2}$ *teaspoon ground nutmeg*
> $\frac{1}{4}$ *teaspoon ground cloves*
> $\frac{1}{3}$ *cup finely chopped citron*
> $\frac{1}{3}$ *cup finely chopped walnuts*
>   2 *tablespoons milk*

Cookie Glaze
>   1 *teaspoon cornstarch*
> $\frac{1}{4}$ *cup confectioners' sugar*
> $\frac{1}{2}$ *cup granulated sugar*
> $\frac{1}{4}$ *cup water*

In a small saucepan, heat the honey just until it simmers. Remove the pan from the heat and set aside to cool.

In a large mixing bowl, beat 1 egg until foamy. Add the sugar, $\frac{1}{4}$ cup at a time, beating well after each addition. Add the honey, the lemon juice, and the grated lemon rind and mix well.

Sift together the flour, baking soda, cinnamon, allspice, nutmeg, and cloves. Blend the sifted ingredients into the honey mixture. Add the citron and the nuts and mix well.

Divide the dough into four parts. Wrap each in foil and chill in the refrigerator overnight.

Preheat the oven to 400°F. Lightly grease cookie sheets with butter. Lightly beat the remaining egg with the milk.

Make the cookie glaze. Sift together the cornstarch and the confectioners' sugar. Set aside. In a saucepan, combine the granulated sugar and the water. Bring to a boil, stirring constantly until the sugar dissolves. Continue boiling until the mixture threads from the spoon (230°F on a candy thermometer). Remove the pan from the heat and gradually stir in the confectioners'-sugar mixture. Set aside.

On a lightly floured surface, roll out one-quarter of the dough to a thickness of $\frac{1}{4}$ inch. (Keep the rest of the dough chilled until ready to use.) Cut the dough using a 2-inch round cookie cutter. Re-roll and cut the scraps.

Place the cookies 1 inch apart on the prepared cookie sheets. Brush each one with the egg and milk mixture. Bake for 10 to 12 minutes, or until no indentations remain on the cookies when touched.

When the lebküchen are removed from the oven, immediately brush them with the glaze. (If the glaze crystallizes while brushing the cookies, warm it over low heat, adding a little water, until it is clear again.) Transfer the cookies to wire racks to cool.

Gingerbread People and Things

Boys and girls, Christmas trees and wreaths, stars and crescent moons—this recipe can be used to make whatever manner of cutout gingerbread cookie you choose. Makes about sixty 6-inch cookies or ninety 3-inch cookies.

> 5 *cups all-purpose flour*
> 1½ *teaspoons baking soda*
> 2 *teaspoons ground ginger*
> 1 *teaspoon ground cinnamon*
> 1 *teaspoon ground cloves*
> ½ *teaspoon salt*
> 1 *cup shortening*
> 1 *cup granulated sugar*
> 1 *egg*
> 1 *cup molasses*
> 2 *tablespoons white vinegar*

Decorative Icing

    1 *egg white*
    2 *teaspoons lemon juice*
$1\frac{1}{2}$–2 *cups confectioners' sugar, sifted*
      Food coloring

Sift together the flour, baking soda, ginger, cinnamon, cloves, and salt.

In a large mixing bowl, beat the shortening until it is soft and smooth. Add the sugar and beat until the mixture is fluffy. Add the egg, molasses, and vinegar. Beat well. Add the flour mixture, $\frac{1}{2}$ cup at a time, beating well after each addition. When the dough is smooth, divide it into quarters. Wrap each portion in foil and chill in the refrigerator for at least 3 hours.

Preheat the oven to 375°F. Grease cookie sheets with butter.

On a lightly floured surface, roll out the dough to a thickness of $\frac{1}{8}$ inch. (Use only one-quarter of the dough at a time and keep the remainder in the refrigerator until you are ready to use it.) Cut the dough with cookie cutters. Re-roll and cut the scraps.

Place the cookies on the cookie sheets. Bake for 5 minutes, or until the cookies are very lightly browned around the edges.

Let the cookies cool on the cookie sheets for 1 minute, then transfer them to wire racks to cool completely.

To make the icing, in a small mixing bowl, beat the egg white, lemon juice, and 1 cup of the confectioners' sugar. Gradually add only enough confectioners' sugar to make an icing of piping consistency. When the consistency seems right, stir in a few drops of food coloring if desired.

To decorate the cookies, fill a decorating bag no more than half full of icing. Use a tip with a small opening. First pipe outlines on the edges of the cookies, then fill in the details.

Stained-Glass Window Cookies

These cookies are so lovely you may want to hang some of them on your Christmas tree. To make cookie ornaments, use a drinking straw to make a hole in the top end of each cookie before baking it. After the cookies have cooled completely, simply thread a piece of yarn through each hole, tying the yarn at the top to make a loop. The hard candy required in this recipe can be sourballs in assorted colors or you may use rolls of ring-shaped candy. Makes about 40 cookies.

> 6 *tablespoons unsalted butter at room temperature*
> $\frac{1}{3}$ *cup shortening*
> $\frac{3}{4}$ *cup granulated sugar*
> 1 *egg*

1 *tablespoon milk*
1 *teaspoon vanilla extract*
2 *cups all-purpose flour*
1½ *teaspoons baking powder*
¼ *teaspoon salt*
4 *ounces hard candy*

In a large mixing bowl, cream together the butter, shortening, and sugar. Beat until light and fluffy. Beat in the egg, the milk, and the vanilla.

Sift together the flour, baking powder, and salt. Add the sifted ingredients, ½ cup at a time, to the batter. Beat until smooth.

Divide the dough in half. Wrap each half in foil and chill in the refrigerator for at least 3 hours.

Preheat the oven to 375°F. Line cookie sheets with foil.

On a lightly floured surface, roll out half the dough to a thickness of ⅛ inch. (Keep the rest of the dough chilled until needed.) Cut with decorative cookie cutters. Re-roll and cut the scraps.

Place the cookies on the lined cookie sheets. Using a sharp knife or tiny hors d'oeuvre cutters, carefully cut out one or more small shapes in the middle of each cookie.

Separate the hard candies by color and put them into plastic bags. Place one bag at a time in a dish towel and, using a hammer or the flat edge of a meat mallet, crush the candy into coarse pieces.

Spoon a little of the candy into the cutout centers of the cookies. Be sure to fill the holes to the level of the dough. (As the cookies bake the candy will melt into smooth windows.)

Bake the cookies for 7 minutes, or until the edges of the cookies are lightly browned and the candy has melted.

Let the cookies cool completely on the cookie sheet, then remove them carefully with a spatula.

Pfeffernüsse

These little treats improve with age. Store the pfeffernüsse in an airtight container for several weeks to allow them to ripen. Before serving, they may be rolled in confectioners' sugar. Makes about 110 cookies.

3 *cups all-purpose flour*
1 *teaspoon baking powder*
$\frac{3}{4}$ *teaspoon salt*
$\frac{1}{2}$ *teaspoon freshly ground black pepper*
1 *teaspoon ground cinnamon*
$\frac{1}{2}$ *teaspoon ground mace*
1 *teaspoon ground allspice*
$\frac{1}{2}$ *cup candied citron, finely chopped*
$\frac{1}{4}$ *cup candied orange peel, finely chopped*
1 *teaspoon grated lemon rind*
3 *eggs*
$1\frac{1}{2}$ *cups granulated sugar*

Preheat the oven to 350°F. Lightly grease cookie sheets with butter.

Into a large mixing bowl, sift together the flour, baking powder, salt, black pepper, cinnamon, mace, and allspice. Add the citron, orange peel, and grated lemon rind and mix well.

In another bowl, combine the eggs and the sugar. Beat until thick and lemon colored. Add to the flour mixture and blend well. If necessary, knead the dough with your hands.

Pinch off small pieces of dough and shape into $\frac{3}{4}$-inch balls. Place them about 1 inch apart on the prepared cookie sheets. Bake for about 15 minutes, or until the bottoms of the cookies are lightly browned.

Candied Kumquats

This sweet-sour little fruit has a unique flavor and makes a delightful confection. Use only firm, brightly colored kumquats.

4 *cups kumquats*
5 *cups water*
$3\frac{1}{2}$ *cups granulated sugar*
$\frac{1}{8}$ *teaspoon cream of tartar*

Wash the kumquats and, using a skewer or a tapestry needle, prick a hole in the stem end of each one.

Put the kumquats into a saucepan and add 4

cups of water. Cook over moderate heat until the water begins to boil. Reduce the heat and simmer the kumquats for 10 minutes.

Drain the kumquats in a colander, then spread them on paper towels to dry.

In a heavy saucepan, combine the remaining cup of water with 2 cups of the sugar. Cook over low heat, stirring constantly, until the sugar is dissolved. Stir in the cream of tartar. Increase the heat to moderate and cook, stirring constantly, until the syrup reaches the soft-ball stage (238°F on a candy thermometer).

Reduce the heat to low, add the kumquats, and let them simmer gently, stirring frequently, for 10 minutes.

Using a perforated spoon, remove the kumquats from the syrup and put them on wire racks to drain and cool.

Spread the remaining $1\frac{1}{2}$ cups of sugar on a plate.

When the kumquats are cool enough to handle, roll each one in the sugar. Return the kumquats to the wire racks to cool completely.

Popcorn Balls

Popcorn balls are fun to make, especially if there are kids around to help. Make tiny balls and heap them in a bowl. Make medium-size or large balls, wrap each one in cellophane gathered at the top with a red or green ribbon, and hang them on the

Christmas tree. About $\frac{1}{2}$ cup of unpopped corn should make the 6 cups of popped corn called for in this recipe.

> 6 *cups popped corn*
> 2 *cups shelled peanuts*
> 1$\frac{1}{2}$ *tablespoons unsalted butter*
> 1$\frac{1}{2}$ *cups firmly packed dark brown sugar*
> 6 *tablespoons water*

Put the popped corn into a large bowl or pot. Add the peanuts. Mix well and set aside.

In a heavy saucepan, melt the butter over low heat. Add the sugar and water and continue cooking over low heat, stirring constantly, until the sugar is dissolved.

Increase the heat to moderate and boil the syrup, without stirring, until it reaches the soft-ball stage (238°F on a candy thermometer).

Slowly pour the hot syrup over the popped corn and peanuts, turning and mixing with a long-handled wooden spools to coat all the kernels and nuts.

As soon as the mixture is cool enough to handle, shape it lightly into balls with buttered hands.

Let the popcorn balls dry thoroughly on waxed paper or a cookie sheet before wrapping them.